QUICK NOTES AND FAST QUOTES FOR EVERY OCCASION

QUICK NOTES AND FAST QUOTES FOR EVERY OCCASION

Jill Williams

Self-Counsel Press
(*a division of*)
International Self-Counsel Press Ltd.
Canada   U.S.A.

Printed in Canada

First edition: September, 1991
Second edition: April, 1992

Canadian Cataloguing in Publication Data
Williams, Jill.
    Quick notes and fast quotes for every occasion

    (Self-counsel series)
    ISBN 0-88908-540-4
    1. Quotations, English.   2. Greeting cards.
3. Wit and Humour.   I. Title.   II. Series.
PN6081.W54 1992   082   C92-091315-6

Cover design adapted from "Strawberry Thief" pattern by William Morris, courtesy of Dover Publications, Inc.

Self-Counsel Press
(*a division of*)
International Self-Counsel Press Ltd.
Head and Editorial Office
1481 Charlotte Road
North Vancouver, British Columbia V7J 1H1

U.S. Address
1704 N. State Street
Bellingham, Washington 98225

CONTENTS

ACKNOWLEDGMENTS

I wish to thank the following people at the Vancouver Public Library who, despite my impatience, took the time to find what I was looking for. From Literature & Language Learning, Judy McIntosh, Thomas Quigley, Pat Richardson, and Jo Anne Tharalson. From Sociology & Sports, Terry Carr, Lou Favelle, and Andrew Martin.

I also want to thank the friends who listened to me read and reread all those "quick notes and fast quotes" over and over again.

And to my most patient listener, Ray Schami.

I would also like to acknowledge my father who taught me the value of saying what you mean in as few words as possible.

A final thanks goes to the people at Self-Counsel Press, especially Ruth Wilson, for their encouragement and support.

INTRODUCTION

**When a thing has been said and said well,
have no scruple. Take it and copy it.**
(Anatole France)

Falling in love. Getting married. Having babies. From birth to death, life is a checkerboard of experiences. And this usually includes some pretty rough times too. Divorce. Illness. Financial difficulties.

What do you say to people who are experiencing these things?

Too often — because it is difficult — we simply don't take the time to do it. We think about it, but the card or note never quite gets written. That's why I wrote this book. To make it a little bit easier.

Now you'll know where to look when you need —

- expressions of sympathy,
- offbeat birthday greetings,
- phrases to add to a congratulatory note,
- romantic words of encouragement,
- work-related messages, and
- get-well wishes.

You'll also find suggestions for —

- how to cancel a wedding — in rhyme,
- a Daylight Savings greeting,
- how to announce the arrival of an adopted child,
- comforting words for the bereaved pet owner, and

- ◆ what to write on a group card when you're the last one to sign.

I've tried as much as possible to include quotations that apply to either sex. But if you come across one you'd like to use that refers to the wrong gender for your purposes, by all means change it! Write "wife" instead of "husband," "father" instead of "mother," whatever is appropriate.

A word about credit. Throughout the book, whenever I suggest a particular quote, I provide the name of the author in parentheses. When the attribution reads *JW*, it's one that I wrote myself. As the author, I am obliged to "give credit where credit is due." But in a personal note, it's the thought that counts, not who first said it.

A QUICK NOTE FROM THE AUTHOR

I offer suggestions, ideas to amuse,
A few apt phrases you may want to use.
And if you use one after you've read it,
You needn't bother to give me credit!

(JW)

LOVE & MARRIAGE

Love is much nicer to be in than an automobile accident, a tight girdle, a higher tax bracket, or a holding pattern over Philadelphia.

(Judith Viorst)

By all means marry; if you get a good wife, you'll become happy; if you get a bad one, you'll become a philosopher.

(Socrates)

A successful marriage requires falling in love many times, always with the same person.

(Mignon McLaughlin)

"I LOVE YOU"

Buy a bag of fortune cookies and remove the "fortunes" from them. Replace them with your own love notes such as the following:

> **You are my good fortune.**
>
> **You're the luck in my life!**
>
> **My future is brighter because you are in it.**

Send a card to your sweetheart with a rainbow on the cover. Inside, write all his or her endearing qualities and compare them with the colors in the rainbow.

> **I love the green of your generosity, the red of your passion, the orange of your laughter, the blue of your gentleness, the yellow of your clever mind. Thank you for being my rainbow.**

Whether you hand your loved one a copy of Elizabeth Barrett Browning's "Sonnet XLIII" ("How do I love thee? Let me count the ways"), or you simply scribble "I LUV U" on a 3 x 5 index card, be creative about where you leave your declaration of love. Stick it on the inside of the bathroom mirror. Tuck it under her pillow. Leave it on an empty plate in the refrigerator. Hide it in his briefcase. If you're feeling especially romantic, attach the following message to a bouquet of balloons:

> **Over the mountains**
> **And under the waves,**
> **Over the fountains**
> **And under the graves,**
> **Over floods which are deepest**
> **Which do Neptune obey,**
> **Over rocks which are steepest**
> **Love will find out the way.**

> *(Anon.)*

2

If you feel more comfortable giving your special friend a traditional flower bouquet, that's okay, too. Here are some love verses you may want to add:

> And all the charms of face or voice
> Which I in others see
> Are but the recollected choice
> Of what I feel for thee.
>
> *(John Clare)*

> A song within a song
> And eyes upon the door—
> And you will always hold me
> One day more.
>
> *(Charles Divine)*

> If you love me as I love you
> What knife can cut our love in two?
>
> *(Rudyard Kipling)*

From a woman to a man:

> How do I love thee? Let me count the ways.
> I love thee to the depth and breadth
>   and height
> My soul can reach when feeling out of sight.
>
> *(Elizabeth Barrett Browning)*

From a man to a woman:

> If I were a king, ah love, if I were a king!
> What tributary nations would I bring
> To stoop before your sceptre and to swear
> Allegiance to your lips and eyes and hair.
>
> *(Justin Huntly McCarthy)*

A DIFFERENT WAY TO SAY "I LOVE YOU"

To add variety to those "three little words" that mean so much in any love relationship, why not try expressing them in another language? You may want to include three or four of the following foreign phrases in a message that reads:

Whether it's Je t'aime (French), Ich liebe dich (German), Ya lublyu tebya (Russian), or Aku cinta padamu (Indonesian), I just want you to know "I LOVE YOU!"

Here are some more to choose from:

Italian:	**Ti amo**
Spanish:	**Te quiero**
Dutch:	**Ik hou van je**
Swedish:	**Jag älskar dig**
Polish:	**Jacie kocham**
Turkish:	**Seni seviyorum**
Cantonese:	**Ngoh oi nei**
Portuguese:	**Eu te amo**

DEFINING THE RELATIONSHIP

It's been a couple of months now. You'd like to know where you stand but you feel awkward asking. A fast way to find out is to send a card with the following question:

What will you be saying about us two years from now?

Or if you feel safer quoting somebody else, try using Samuel Taylor Coleridge's words on the front of the card:

And in today already walks tomorrow,

with this message inside:

How do you feel about that in terms of *us*?

For those of you who *know* how you feel and want your partner to know too, how about personalizing a nursery rhyme:

Roses are red,
Violets are blue
I'm falling in love
How about you?

Or:

Roses are red,
Violets are blue
Pasta's [*fill in favorite food*] delicious
And so are you!

For you non-rhyming romantics:

Every day in every way it's getting better!
Thank you for brightening my life.

MOVING IN TOGETHER

You probably won't need to borrow Christopher Marlowe's "Come live with me and be my love" to get your lover to move in with you. But you might consider the meaning of the Jamaican saying that goes "'Come see me' is one t'ing, but 'come lib wid me' is another" before you make any final decisions! However, there will be other couples who do live together and here are a few thoughts on what to write them in a congratulatory note:

> **Heard the news, I think it's great!**
> **You both deserve to cohabitate!**
>
> *(JW)*

> **Every step is an end, and every step is a fresh**
> **beginning.**
>
> *(Johann Wolfgang von Goethe)*

> **If you are living with a man, you don't have**
> **to worry about whether you should sleep**
> **with him after dinner.**
>
> *(Stephanie Brush)*

> **Come, my friends,**
> **Tis not too late to seek a new world.**
>
> *(Alfred, Lord Tennyson)*

> **They say two can live as cheaply as one.**
> **Now you guys'll have a chance to prove it.**
> **Good luck and congratulations!**

ENGAGEMENT CONGRATULATIONS

Remember this — that very little is needed to make a happy life.

(Marcus Aurelius)

No road is long with good company.

(Proverb)

The Eskimos had 52 names for snow because it was important to them: there ought to be as many for love.

(Margaret Atwood)

The most important thing in a relationship between a man and a woman is that one of them be good at taking orders.

(Linda Festa)

Here's hoping she's [you're] not just a passing fiancée!

(Alfred McFote)

It's never too late to die or get married.

(Yiddish proverb)

They say diamonds are forever. Here's to your love lasting even longer!

It's a big step. Maybe even a little scary. But you both deserve a lifetime of happiness and I'm sure you'll make it happen.

A CLEVER WAY TO CANCEL A WEDDING

If you are ever in the position of having to cancel an engage-
ment or wedding, you may just want to have a tactful friend
call all your guests and let them know that plans have
changed. But here is an announcement for a good-humored
break-off:

> Today you'll find a greeting card for every
>   known occasion,
> From quitting smokes, to growing old, to
>   having a nice vacation.
> Alas, the one both [name] and I have
>   searched in vain to find
> Is the card that says: "The wedding's off,
>   we've had a change of mind."
> So don't send gifts, don't send bread,
>   don't send a loving cup.
> And for heaven's sake, on [wedding date],
>   don't, please DON'T show up!
>
> *(JW)*

MEANINGFUL MARRIAGE MESSAGES

Love is patient and kind; love is not jealous or boastful; it is not arrogant or rude. Love does not insist on its own way; it is not irritable or resentful; it does not rejoice at wrong, but rejoices in the right. Love bears all things, believes all things, hopes all things, endures all things. Love never ends.

(1 Cor. 13:4-8a)

To say the words "love and compassion" is easy. But to accept that love and compassion are built upon patience and perseverance is not easy. Your marriage will be firm and lasting if you remember this.

(Buddhist marriage homily)

There are three sights which warm my heart and are beautiful in the eyes of the Lord and of men: concord among brothers, friendship among neighbors, and a man and wife who are inseparable.

(The Wisdom of Ben Sira)

though love be a day and life be nothing, it shall not stop kissing.

(e.e. cummings)

It is when you give of yourself that you truly give.

(Kahlil Gibran)

Two things do prolong thy life:
A quiet heart and a loving wife.

(Proverb)

The greatest thing you'll ever learn
Is just to love and be loved in return.

(Eden Abba)

Now that you are getting married, there are just two rules to keep in mind:
#1 Don't sweat the small stuff.
#2 It's *all* small stuff!

The best piece of advice I ever heard on how to make a marriage work was this: Never go to bed angry with your mate. (It's a good idea to take turns with the T.V. channel changer, too!)

Here's to the perfect wedding: A beautiful bride, a handsome groom, and a cake with no calories!

For those who elope:

There are just some things no one can do alone: conspire, be a mob, or a choir, or a regiment. Or elope.

(Renata Adler)

To a May/December couple:

While there's snow on the roof, it doesn't mean the fire has gone out in the furnace.

(John G. Diefenbaker)

TRADITIONAL
ANNIVERSARY GIFTS

Whether you use a proverb, an updated song lyric, or a quote from Shakespeare, the gift you give a couple celebrating their anniversary will help you decide what to write on the accompanying card.

Anniversary	Symbol
1st	Paper
2nd	Cotton
3rd	Leather
4th	Books, fruit, flowers
5th	Wood (or clocks)
6th	Iron (or candy)
7th	Copper, bronze, brass, wool
8th	Electrical appliances
9th	Pottery
10th	Tin, aluminum
11th	Steel
12th	Silk, linen
13th	Lace
14th	Ivory
15th	Crystal
20th	China
25th	Silver
30th	Pearl
35th	Jade (or coral)
40th	Ruby
45th	Sapphire
50th	Gold
55th	Emerald
60th	Diamond
75th	Diamond

GREETINGS FOR WEDDING ANNIVERSARIES

1st anniversary (paper):

> **Here's to paper moons**
> **Hung on cardboard skies!**
> **You made it through an entire year**
> **And you still have love in your eyes!**
>
> *(JW)*

5th anniversary (wood):

> **Touch wood, it's sure to come good.**
>
> *(Proverb)*

10th anniversary (tin or aluminum):

> **What metal more attractive**
> **Than love and wedded bliss?**
> **Happy 10th anniversary!**
> **Here's to many more years like this!**
>
> *(JW, with apologies to Shakespeare)*

20th anniversary (china):

> **There's a joy without canker or cark,**
> **There's a pleasure eternally new,**
> **'Tis to gloat on the glaze and the mark**
> **Of china that's ancient and blue.**
>
> *(Andrew Lang)*

25th anniversary (silver):

> **"Darling, am I growing old?**
> **With silver threads among the gold?"**
> **"No," he/she answers, swift and fast.**
> **(And that's what makes their marriage last!)**
>
> *(JW)*

30th anniversary (pearl):

> **Again, the kingdom of heaven is like a merchant looking for fine pearls. When he found one of great value, he went away and sold everything he had and bought it.**
>
> *(Matt. 13:45-46)*

40th anniversary (ruby):

> **The glowing ruby should adorn**
> **Those who in warm July are born,**
> **Then will they be exempt and free**
> **From love's doubt and anxiety.**
>
> **And also rubies should adorn**
> **Those who wake up on this morn**
> **Brushing back the happy tears**
> **That say: "I'm married 40 years!"**
>
> *(JW, inspired by* Notes and Queries,
> *11/May, 1889)*

50th anniversary (gold):

> **Dawn love is silver**
> **Wait for the west:**
> **Old love is gold love —**
> **Old love is best.**
>
> *(Katherine Lee Bates)*

60th anniversary (diamond):

> **Twinkle, twinkle lovely star,**
> **Thank you for the gem you are!**
> **Up above the world so high,**
> **You're the diamond in my sky!**
>
> *(JW)*

75th anniversary (diamond):

> **Character is the diamond that scratches every other stone.**
>
> *(Proverb)*

On any wedding anniversary:

> **As your wedding ring wears, your cares will wear away.**
>
> *(Proverb)*

> **Thank you for proving that some people do in fact marry and live "happily ever after."**

And for a couple that has been married for a long time:

> **I know vows are sacred, but this is ridiculous! Happy anniversary!**

WHEN A RELATIONSHIP ENDS

When a relationship ends, it hurts. Here are some sensitive words from Kahlil Gibran that you might consider including in a note to someone going through this experience:

> **Your pain is the breaking of the shell that encloses your passion.**

> **If the other person injures you, you may forget the injury; but if you injure him, you will always remember.**

> **If it is fear you would dispel, the seat of that fear is in your heart and not in the hand of the feared.**

On a lighter note, here's the perfect pick-me-up for a woman whose lover has just left her:

> **Time wounds all heels.**
>
> *(Jane Ace)*

Not all relationships end unhappily. Some break-ups, in fact, are a welcome relief to both parties! Here are a few choice quotes you might want to scribble to someone in a situation like this:

> **The happiest time of anyone's life is just after the first divorce.**
>
> *(John Kenneth Galbraith)*

> **If a thing is worth doing, it is worth doing badly.**
>
> *(G.K. Chesterton)*

> **Freedom is nothing else but a chance to be better.**
>
> *(Albert Camus)*

And when you're the one doing the breaking up:

> Just because everything is different doesn't mean anything has changed.
>
> *(Irene Poter)*

> My name is Might-have-been; I am also called No-more, Too-late, Farewell.
>
> *(Dante Gabriel Rossetti)*

> We all have reasons for moving. I move to keep things whole.
>
> *(Mark Strand)*

> There's nothing wrong with you. It's the relationship that wasn't working. Hang in there.

THE SECOND TIME AROUND

For those who marry more than once — whether after a divorce or because of being widowed:

> **The present is the only thing that has no end.**
>
> *(Erwin Schrodinger)*

> **Be happy. It's one way of being wise.**
>
> *(Colette)*

> **Time in love and time in life are unrelated: forever exists more than once.**
>
> *(Ned Rorem)*

> **A man without a wife is like a vase without flowers.**
>
> *(African proverb)*

> **Whether it's playing tennis or getting married, practice makes perfect. Here's to number [2, 3, 4, *or whatever number marriage it is*] being a winner!**

For older newlyweds:

> **The best is yet to be,**
> **The last of life, for which the first was**
> **made....**
>
> *(Robert Browning)*

> **To see a young couple loving each other is no wonder; but to see an old couple loving each other is the best sight of all.**
>
> *(William Makepeace Thackeray)*

QUICK NOTES ON
LOVE & MARRIAGE

Here are some general greetings for couples who are either about to be married or have already been married for a few years and are still very much in love:

May the path you've chosen to travel together be filled with wonderful surprises.

Here's my wish for the two of you:
A lifetime of dreams that all come true!

In big ways and in small ways, may love be with you always.

Today is just the beginning.

Watching the two of you together has made me believe in fairy tales again!

BIRTHS & BIRTHDAYS

To heir is human.
(Dolores E. McGuire)

Born on Monday,
Fair in face;
Born on Tuesday,
Full of God's grace;
Born on Wednesday,
Sour and sad;
Born on Thursday,
Merry and glad;
Born on Friday,
Worthily given;
Born on Saturday,
Work hard for your living;
Born on Sunday,
You will never know want.
(Anon.)

Anyone can get old. All you have to do is live long enough.
(Groucho Marx)

ANNOUNCING A PREGNANCY
꧁

More and more parents-to-be are celebrating the early announcement of a pregnancy. If you are among this group, the following rhymes might save you time and explanations:

> Hip, hip, hooray!
> We're expecting in May!
>
> Next Christmas 'neath the tree,
> There'll be [*mother*] and [*father*]
> And baby makes three!
> (Just wanted to let you know.)
>
> Could be Aries!
> Could be Taurus!
> [*fill in appropriate astrological sign*]
> The birth date is still a "Big Maybe."
> No matter which sign
> We're feeling divine
> Now that we're having a baby!
>
> *(JW)*

GREETINGS FOR MOTHERS-TO-BE
꧁

Oh what a tangled web we weave
When first we practice to conceive.

(Don Herrold)

The beginning is the most important part of the work.

(Plato)

Things are not as quickly achieved as conceived.

(Yiddish proverb)

If pregnancy were a book, they would cut the last two chapters.

(Nora Ephron)

20

YOU DON'T NEED AN UMBRELLA TO WRITE
GOOD BABY SHOWER NOTES

You've got the gift — now it's time to enclose the note. Here's a multiple choice baby shower message that ought to help you get started:

> **Dear [*name*],**
>
> **I am so_____[thrilled about/excited by/ happy with/delighted over] the_____ [good news/latest development/incredible update] that I_____[couldn't resist/had to rush out and buy/simply wanted to give you] this [*describe gift item*] as a way of saying_____ ["Be well and be happy!"/"Mazel tov!"/ Here's to motherhood — and you!", "Health and Happiness to you both!"]**
>
> **_____[God bless/All the best/With great affection]**

BIRTH ANNOUNCEMENTS

The traditional way of announcing the arrival of a newborn is to include the baby's full name, date of birth, the names of the parents, and the place the baby was born. But if you want to be a bit different, here are several suggestions:

From the proud parents of a baby daughter:

> **We have skirted the issue.**
>
> *(Earl Wilson)*

> **Thank heaven, for little girls**
> **For little girls get bigger ev'ry day**
> **Thank heaven, for little girls**
> **They grow up in the most delightful way!**
>
> *(Alan Jay Lerner)*

And for the birth of a boy:

> **Joy of joy, it's a [*baby's weight*] boy!**

For twins:

> **There is two things in this life for which we are never fully prepared, and that is — twins.**
>
> *(Josh Billings)*

> **When one starts crying**
> **The other begins;**
> **And nobody can find**
> **Enough safety pins.**
> **Oh, they said we'd have a baby, but**
> **A baby isn't twins!**
>
> *(Dorothy Aldis)*

A fun way to announce multiple births:

> **Wot in hell have we done to deserve all these kittens?**
>
> *(Don Marquis)*

Should you decide to include the infant's photo in the birth announcement, here are some possible captions:

> **Sleep she as sound as careless infancy.**
>
> *(Shakespeare)*

> **A source of innocent merriment.**
>
> *(W.S. Gilbert)*

> **Small is beautiful.**
>
> *(E.F. Schumacher)*

> **...a face like a benediction.**
>
> *(Cervantes)*

> **Every baby born into the world is finer than the last.**
>
> *(Charles Dickens)*

> **Large streams from little fountains flow, Tall oaks from little acorns grow.**
>
> *(David Everett)*

Especially good for a yawning (or crying) infant:

> **Out of the mouths of babes and sucklings hast thou ordained strength.**
>
> *(Psalm 8:2)*

ANNOUNCING THE ARRIVAL
OF AN ADOPTED CHILD

In certain situations, where there are no set rules to follow, I would encourage you to *do what you feel like doing*. If, for example, you've adopted a child and want to share your good news with family and friends but aren't sure what to write on the announcement, try one of these:

> Where did you come from, baby dear?
> Out of the Everywhere into here.
> > *(George McDonald)*

> [*Adoption date*]
> We are proud and pleased to announce the arrival of our adopted son/daughter [*child's name*].

> "Seek and ye shall find."
> We're blessed because we did.
> On [*date of adoption*] we adopted [*name*].
> He's/She's one terrific kid!
> > *(JW)*

> The Age of Miracles, as it ever was, now is.
> > *(Thomas Carlyle)*

> (Our "miracle" is named [*child's name*]
> Adopted: [*date*])

To acknowledge the adopted child's arrival:

> May [*child's name*] be sprinkled from morning to night with the dew of grace.
> > *(Rufus Jones)*

> A babe in a house is a well-spring of pleasure.
> > *(Martin Tupper)*

BIRTH CONGRATULATIONS

Congratulations. We all knew you had it in you.

(Dorothy Parker)

A bit of talcum
Is always walcum.

(Ogden Nash)

Babies are such a nice way to start people.
(Don Herrold)

Sweet babe, in thy face
Soft desires I can trace,
Secret joys and secret smiles,
Little pretty infant wiles.

(William Blake)

How beautifully everything is arranged by
Nature; as soon as a child enters the world,
it finds a mother ready to take care of it.
(Jules Michelet)

A baby will make love stronger, days
shorter, nights longer, bankroll smaller,
home happier, clothes shabbier, the past
forgotten, and the future worth living for.
(Anon.)

When the first baby laughed for the first
time, the laugh broke into a million pieces,
and they all went skipping about. That was
the beginning of fairies.

(Sir James M. Barrie)

Caption for a newborn feeding from a bottle:

There's a sucker born every minute!
(P.T. Barnum)

CHRISTENING NOTES

The following poem provides a nice way to acknowledge a baby's christening. To personalize it, add the words: "**Unlike** [*baby's name*]" at the beginning:

> **When I was christened**
> **they held me up**
> **and poured some water**
> **out of a cup.**
>
> **The trouble was**
> **it fell on me,**
> **and I and water**
> **don't agree.**
>
> **A lot of christeners**
> **stood and listened:**
> **I let them know**
> **that I was christened!**
>
> *(David McCord)*
>
> **(May the blessings of this special day be with you always.)**

An offbeat message for a male child:

> **Why call your son Arthur? Every Tom, Dick and Harry is called Arthur!**
> *(Samuel Goldwyn)*

(Note: You may substitute any name for "Arthur" except, of course, "Tom," "Dick," or "Harry.")

HOW TO SAY
"HAPPY BIRTHDAY!"
IN 16 DIFFERENT LANGUAGES

Suggested greeting:

I wish you "Otanjyobi Omedeto!" (Japanese), "Buon Compleanno!" (Italian), "Penblwydd hapus!" (Welsh). Or, if you have to have it spelled out in plain English, "Happy Birthday!"

(See below for more choices.)

Arabic:	Eed Melad Saïd
Chinese, Cantonese:	Sāang Yaht faai lokik
Croatian:	Sretan Rodjen Dan
Danish:	Hjertelig til lykke med- fødselsdagen
Dutch:	Hartelijk gefeliciteerd met- je verjaardag
Finnish:	Onneksi Olkoon
French:	Bonne fête
German:	Herzlichen Glückwunsch zum Geburtstag
Hungarian:	Boldog Szuletes Napot
Russian:	Sdnyom rozhdenya
Spanish:	Feliz Cumpleaños
Thai:	Suksan Wankerd
Turkish:	Dogūn günün kutlu olsun

GENERAL BIRTHDAY GREETINGS

Birthday wishes are a dime a dozen.
For a maiden aunt or long lost cousin.
This one's different! This one's new!
It's sent to a winner: Namely YOU!

You're always doing special things for
everybody else. Today is your special
day! Have a good one!

Many Happy Returns! (Where have you
been, anyway?)

I'd buy you a cake but I'm on a diet
I'd set off a rocket but I like things quiet
I'd gift-wrap a Rolls but cars aren't
my thing:
So I guess I'll just say the same damn
old thing:
Have a REALLY GREAT BIRTHDAY!

(JW)

A BIRTHDAY REBUS FOR A CHILD

A rebus is a puzzle consisting of pictures. Kids love them. So the next time a "little person" you know is celebrating a birthday, why not create a birthday rebus?

 (Name), HOPE YOU HAVE

A 1-DERFUL BIRTHDAY WITH LOTS OF

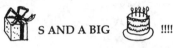 S AND A BIG !!!!

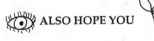 ALSO HOPE YOU

UNDERSTAND THIS !!!!

 LOVE,

16th BIRTHDAY GREETINGS

Sixteen candles make a lovely light
But not as bright as your eyes tonight.
(Luther Dixon)

Your flag's unfurled
You're a woman of the world
Cuz you're sweet sixteen.

(Roger Eden)

You've crossed an important threshold:
Adulthood has almost begun...
But please don't grow up too quickly
This is the time to have fun!

(JW)

21st BIRTHDAY GREETINGS

With a little rewrite, A.E. Houseman's "When I Was One-And-Twenty" works as a birthday greeting for either sex:

> When I was all of twenty
> I heard a wise man say,
> "Give crowns and pounds and guineas
> But not your heart away;
> Give pearls away and rubies
> But keep your fancy free."
> But I was all of twenty
> No use to talk to me.
>
> When I was all of twenty
> I heard him say again,
> "The heart out of the bosom
> Was never given in vain;
> 'Tis paid with sighs a plenty
> And sold for endless rue."
> Well I am one-and-twenty now
> And oh, 'tis true, 'tis true.

At 21, so many things appear solid, permanent, untenable.

(Orson Welles)

It's not easy to achieve freedom without chaos.

(Anaïs Nin)

30th BIRTHDAY

Time and tide wait for no man — but time always stands still for a woman of 30.

(Robert Frost)

Men make love more intensely at 20, but make love better, however, at 30.

(Catherine the Great)

When you turn 30, a whole new thing happens: you see yourself acting like your parents.

(Blair Sabol)

Women over thirty are at their best, but men over thirty are too old to recognize it.

(Jean-Paul Belmondo)

40th BIRTHDAY

The lovely thing about being 40 is that you can appreciate 25-year-old men.

(Colleen McCullough)

When a man is past 40 and does not become a crook, he is either feeble-minded or a genius.

(Lin Yutang)

The best years are the forties; after 50 a man begins to deteriorate, but in the forties he is at the maximum of his villainy.

(H.L. Mencken)

Be wise with speed;
A fool at forty is a fool indeed.

(Edward Young)

50th BIRTHDAY

To compliment someone on their 50th birthday, quote George Orwell's:

> **At 50, everyone has the face he deserves.**
>
> **(Happy Birthday, Handsome! or Happy Birthday, Gorgeous!)**

> **A man's beginning his prime at fifty, or there never was much man in him.**
>
> *(George Meredith)*

> **I know a lot of men [women] who are healthier at age 50 than they've ever been before because a lot of their fear is gone.**
>
> *(Robert Bly)*

> **You have everything now you had 20 years ago — except now it's all lower.**
>
> *(Gypsy Rose Lee)*

> **The secret of staying young is to live honestly, eat slowly, and lie about your age.**
>
> *(Lucille Ball)*

FOR THOSE TURNING 60 PLUS

Age cannot wither her
Nor custom stale her infinite variety...
(Shakespeare)

Is not old wine wholesomest, old pippins toothsomest, old wood burn brightest, old linen wash whitest? Old soldiers, sweet-hearts, are surest, and old lovers are sound-est.
(John Webster)

Living well is the best revenge.
(George Herbert)

Time, which changes people, does not alter the image we have retained of them.
(Marcel Proust)

Old age has its pleasures, which, though different, are not less than the pleasures of youth.
(W. Somerset Maugham)

The longer I live the more I see that I am never wrong about anything, and that all the pains I have so humbly taken to verify my notions have only wasted my time.
(George Bernard Shaw)

Autumn is mellower, and what we lose in flowers, we more than gain in fruits.
(Samuel Butler)

MORE BIRTHDAY GREETINGS
FOR THE OLDER PERSON

Let us cherish and love old age, for it is full of pleasure if we know how to use it.

(Seneca)

As I approve of a youth that has something of the old man in him, so I am no less pleased with an old man that has something of the youth. He that follows this rule may be old in body, but can never be so in mind.

(Cicero)

Old age has a great sense of calm and freedom. When the passions have relaxed their hold, you have escaped not from one master but from many.

(Plato)

As the clear light is upon the holy candlestick; so is the beauty of the face in ripe age.

(Eccles.)

King Solomon and King David
Led very merry lives.
With very many concubines
And very many wives,
Until old age came creeping,
With very many qualms,
Then Solomon wrote the Proverbs,
And David wrote the Psalms.

(Anon.)

34

ASTROLOGICAL
BIRTHDAY CHART

Astrology is great for saying "Happy Birthday!" in a slightly different way. Next time someone you know is having a birthday, why not cut out the appropriate "astrological forecast" from your local newspaper and include it with the card? Here's a chart to help you match birthdays and zodiac signs.

♒	**AQUARIUS:**	January 21 - February 19
♓	**PISCES:**	February 20 - March 20
♈	**ARIES:**	March 21 - April 20
♉	**TAURUS:**	April 21 - May 21
♊	**GEMINI:**	May 22 - June 21
♋	**CANCER:**	June 22 - July 23
♌	**LEO:**	July 24 - August 23
♍	**VIRGO:**	August 24 - September 23
♎	**LIBRA:**	September 24 - October 23
♏	**SCORPIO:**	October 24 - November 22
♐	**SAGITTARIUS:**	November 23 - December 21
♑	**CAPRICORN:**	December 22 - January 20

BELATED BIRTHDAY GREETINGS

I've a grand memory for forgetting.
(Robert Louis Stevenson)

From a remorseful husband:

> **The best way to remember your wife's birthday is to forget it once.**
>
> *(H.V. Prochnow)*

> **(Sorry, hon. It won't happen again until next year!)**

THE PERFECT QUOTE FOR THE PERFECT GIFT

For a plant:

> **All the great pleasures in life are silent.**
> *(George Clemenceau)*

For a sports car:

> **Power is the great aphrodisiac.**
> *(Henry Kissinger)*

For perfume or a bottle of booze:

> **That which does not kill me makes me stronger.**
>
> *(Friedrich Nietzsche)*

For an umbrella:

> **Into each life some rain must fall.**
> *(Henry Wadsworth Longfellow)*

PICKING THE RIGHT PEN

Whether you prefer a fountain, ballpoint, felt tip, or roller ball pen, notes are a lot more fun to write and receive when they can be read easily. When you're scripting something on one of those very glossy greeting cards, I recomend a felt tip pen with permanent ink, medium to fine point. Although most pens come in four basic colors — black, blue, green, and red — the most popular color is black. When you're writing a note on colored paper, use a paint marker with a very fine point. Why not pick one that writes in gold so you can dazzle the recipient with your visual as well as your verbal brilliance!

THE CONSIDERATE GIFT-GIVER

When the gift you give is an article of clothing, or something that is easily returnable, it's nice to include that bit of information in the accompanying note along with the receipt. (Believe me, the person getting the gift will appreciate this considerate gesture far more than how much money you've spent.) Write the following in a P.S. and clip or tape the receipt to the back of the card:

> **P.S. If this isn't right for you, please feel free to exchange it for something else. (I've included the receipt to make it easier.)**

QUICK NOTES FOR BIRTHDAYS

For the person you don't really know that well (a distant relative, the new receptionist at work, your son's favorite teacher, etc.), here are some general birthday greetings you may want to use.

Because you are a very special person, you deserve a special day all your own. Happy birthday!

A wish for today: May every one of your wishes come true. (Forget about blowing out all the candles on the cake. That's an old wives' tale, anyway!) Have a good one!

Did you know that Beethoven and Oprah Winfrey are Sagittarians too? Happy birthday!

(Choose appropriate names from the list below.)

David Letterman/Joan Crawford	Aries
William Shakespeare/Barbra Streisand	Taurus
Bob Dylan/Marilyn Monroe	Gemini
Rembrandt/Princess Di	Cancer
George Bernard Shaw/Madonna	Leo
Jimmy Connors/Ingrid Bergman	Virgo
Miguel Cervantes/Barbara Walters	Libra
Johnny Carson/Marie Antoinette	Scorpio
Beethoven/Oprah Winfrey	Sagittarius
Benjamin Franklin/Elizabeth Arden	Capricorn
Wayne Gretzky/Colette	Aquarius
Michaelangelo/Elizabeth Taylor	Pisces

FAMILY & FRIENDS

The family is one of nature's masterpieces.

> *(George Santayana)*

Birds in their little nest
  agree;
And 'tis a shameful sight,
When children of one
  family
Fall out, and chide, and
  fight.

> *(Isaac Watts)*

A friend in need is a friend
to be avoided.

> *(Lord Samuel)*

HOLIDAY GREETINGS:
A GREAT WAY TO COMMUNICATE

Whether you're celebrating a religious holiday or you just want to say "Hi!" to a friend in an off-beat way, there are numerous times throughout the year when holiday greetings, along with an appropriate message, are a great way to communicate.

HAPPY NEW YEAR!

New Year's Day is every man's birthday.
(Charles Lamb)

Now the New Year reviving old Desires,
The thoughtful Soul to Solitude retires.
(Edward Fitzgerald)

Ring out the old, ring in the new,
Ring, happy bells, across the snow:
The year is going, let him go;
Ring out the false, ring in the true.
(Alfred, Lord Tennyson)

GROUNDHOG DAY

Sending cards on little-known or never-acknowledged holidays is a great way to renew contact with someone you've lost track of. It's also a good way of initiating friendships, romantic or otherwise.

Happy Groundhog Day! ...And speaking of coming out of hibernation, when are we going to get together? Soon, I hope!

VALENTINE'S DAY

Awake my heart, to be loved, awake, awake!
(Robert Bridges)

Love does not consist in gazing at each other but in looking together in the same direction.
(Saint Exupéry)

Love is a sweet tyranny, because the lover endureth his torments willingly.
(Proverb)

How wise are they that are but fools in love!
(Joshua Cooke)

From a loving wife:

> Some pray to marry the man they love,
> My prayer will somewhat vary:
> I humbly pray to Heaven above
> That I love the man I marry.
> *(Rose Pastor Stokes)*

> (And I do! Happy Valentine's Day, my love.)

From a devoted husband:

> I that have love and no more
> Give you but love of you, sweet;
> He that hath more, let him give;
> He that hath wings, let him soar;
> Mine is the heart at your feet
> Here, that must love you to live.
> *(Algernon Charles Swinburne)*

A Valentine greeting for someone not romantically inclined:

> If love is the answer, could you rephrase the question?
> *(Lily Tomlin)*

41

SAINT PATRICK'S DAY

Whether you're Irish or not, Saint Patrick's Day is one fun holiday! Be sure to use green ink on white paper when you include one of these "shamrocks" in your card:

> Oh, the music in the air!
> An' the joy that's ivrywhere —
> Shure, the whole blue vault o'heaven is
>   wan grand triumphal arch;
> An' the earth below is gay,
> Wid its tender green th'-day,
> For the whole world is Irish on the Seven-
>   teenth o' March.
>
> *(Daly)*

THE BEST PAT

> St. Patrick's Day brings to mind
> Other Pats of a varied kind.
> Pat-pending is found everywhere;
> Go where you will, you'll find him there.
> Pat-rimony, no matter when,
> Is warmly welcomed by the men.
> We find the sellers of any stage
> Are very fond of Pat-ronage.
> There's a Pat the ladies use —
> Pat-tern, when to sew they choose.
> But to our favorite we'll stick —
> Beloved of old, St. Pat—rick.
>
> *(Anon.)*

A message to an Irish playboy on St. Patrick's Day:

> **They say Saint Patrick's best-known mira-
> cle was to banish all poisonous snakes from
> Ireland. I guess one got away.**
>
> *(JW)*

A DAYLIGHT SAVINGS GREETING

For those of you who are into little-known facts about lesser-known holidays, here's one for you: Can you name the person who is known as the originator of the Daylight Savings system? William Willett. How about the first nation to use it? Germany. The year was 1915 and it was used in order to conserve on fuel and power. For your purposes, however, it gives you a delightful excuse to communicate with someone you haven't been in touch with lately.

On the front of a card that features either clocks or sunlight, write **Happy Daylight Savings**! Inside, add the following:

> **Are you confused about clocks?**
> **Which way you're supposed to set 'em?**
> **It's "Spring forward and Fall behind."**
> **So relax now [*name*] and forget 'em!**
>
> *(JW)*

EASTER OR SPRING GREETINGS

For Easter:

> Spring bursts today,
> For Christ is risen and all the earth's at play.
> *(Christina Rossetti)*

> Twas Easter Sunday. The full-blossomed
>   trees
> Filled all the air with fragrance and with
>   joy.
> *(Henry Wadsworth Longfellow)*

A simple **Alleluia!** says it all, too.

For Spring:

> Now the woods are in leaf, now the year is
> in its greatest beauty.
> *(Vergil)*

> Gentle Spring! In sunshine clad,
> Well dost thou thy power display!
> *(Charles D'Orleans)*

> It is the month of June,
> The month of leaves and roses,
> When pleasant sights salute the eyes,
> And pleasant scents the noses.
> *(Nathaniel Parker Willis)*

A spring greeting for someone who appreciates a different kind of greenery:

> Spring is here, — and I could be very happy,
> except that I am broke.
> *(Edna St. Vincent Millay)*

MOTHER'S DAY

Mothers of the race, the most important actors in the grand drama of human progress.
(Elizabeth Cady Stanton)

Now, as always, the most automated appliance in a household is the mother.
(Beverly Johnson)

The mother! She is what keeps the family intact...it is proved. A fact.
(Anna F. Trevisan)

Who inuhell wants to try to make pies like Mother makes when it's so much simpler to let Mother make um inu first place.
(Harriette Arnow)

You're just the splendidest, goodest mamsie in all the world. And I'm a hateful cross old bear, so I am!
(Margaret Sidney)

Remarkable women of older times are like ancient painted glass — the art of making them is lost.
(Harriet Beecher Stowe)

FATHER'S DAY

Let us now praise famous men, and our fathers that begat us.

(Eccles.)

You don't have to deserve your mother's love. You have to deserve your father's. He's more particular.

(Ben Johnson)

There is something ultimate in a father's love, something that cannot fail, something to be believed against the whole world.

(Frederick W. Faber)

It is a wise father that knows his own child.

(Shakespeare)

(Thanks, Dad, for knowing me so well.)

From a woman to the man who is being a father to her children:

It is easier for a father to have children than for children to have a real father.

(Pope John XXIII)

(Thanks for always being there when they need you.)

46

4th OF JULY

A conundrum for Independence Day:

Why is the Fourth of July like oysters?
Because we can't enjoy it without crackers.
Happy Independence Day!

THANKSGIVING

Come, ye thankful people, come
Raise the song of Harvest-home.
(Henry Alford)

So once in every year we throng
Upon a day apart,
To praise the Lord with feast and song
In thankfulness of heart.
(Arthur Guiterman)

This is the sum total of Thanksgiving lore:
Not to be thankful until you're tired of
what you're being thankful for.
(Ogden Nash)

SEASON'S GREETINGS

Such a winter eve. Now for a mellow fire,
some old poet's page, or else serene philos-
ophy.

(Henry David Thoreau)

Better the chill blast of winter than the hot
breath of a pursuing elephant.

(Chinese proverb)

Let's dance and sing and make good cheer,
For Christmas comes but once a year.

(G. MacFarren)

I love the Christmas-tide and yet,
I notice this each year I live;
I always like the gifts I get,
But how I love the gifts I give!

(Carolyn Wells)

As you light each Chanukah candle,
And watch your children's faces,
Pray for understanding
Among people of all races.

(JW)

Holidays are an expensive trial of strength.
The only satisfaction comes from survival.

(Jonathan Miller)

FOR SPECIAL FRIENDSHIPS

The reward of friendship is itself. The man who hopes for anything else does not understand what true friendship is.

(Saint Ailred of Rievaulx)

A good friend is my nearest relation.

(Proverb)

Friendship needs no words — it is solitude delivered from the anguish of loneliness.

(Dag Hammarskjold)

The truth is friendship is to me every bit as sacred and eternal as marriage.

(Katherine Mansfield)

GENERAL FAMILY GREETINGS

Without a family, man alone in the world, trembles with the cold.

(Andre Maurois)

Father, Mother and Me,
Sister and Auntie say
All the people like us are We,
And everyone else is They.

(Rudyard Kipling)

The family you come from isn't as important as the family you're going to have.

(Ring Lardner)

I'M SORRY

For those times when you say or do something you regret, I recommend adding one of the following quotes to an "I'm Sorry" card:

> **In every pardon there is love.**
>
> *(Welsh proverb)*

> **If we are to love others as we love ourselves, then we must learn to love the little self which so often needs to be forgiven for doing the things we do not want to do and saying the things we do not want to say.**
>
> *(Rebecca Beard)*

> **To err is human,**
> **To forgive takes restraint;**
> **To forget you forgave**
> **Is the mark of a saint.**
>
> *(Suzanne Douglass)*

Another way to make amends is by enclosing a sprig of rue (thyme is just as good) in your note and writing:

> **I rue the day I hurt you**
> **And pray that thyme will mend**
> **The distance I created**
> **Between you and me, my friend.**
>
> *(JW)*

FOREIGN LANGUAGE APOLOGIES

Apologizing isn't always easy. But here is an approach you may want to take the next time you need to say "I'm sorry."

It's hard for me to say "I'm sorry." in any language. But how about if I said it in German? Entschuldigung!

(Use whichever language you like.)

Cantonese:	**Deui mjyuh**
Finnish:	**Anteeksi**
French:	**Je regrette**
Indonesian:	**Maaf**
Italian:	**Mi dispiace**
Japanese:	**Sumimasen**
Korean:	**Joe song ham ni da**
Norwegian:	**Forlat meg**
Spanish:	**Lo siento**
Thai:	**Kaw toht**
Turkish:	**Afedersiniz**
Yugoslavian:	**Zao mi je**

QUICK NOTE FOR
FAMILY OCCASIONS

- COME ONE COME ALL!
  WE'RE GONNA HAVE A BALL!

- HERE'S THE PLAN:
  A GATHERING OF THE CLAN!

- IT'S PARTY TIME! COME JOIN
  US!

Dear [*name*],

We're having a ___ [family reunion/Thanks-giving feast/birthday picnic] at ___ [*time*] am/pm on _____[*date*] at _____ [*location*]. It would mean _____ [an awful lot to all of us/so much to me personally/everything to the kids] if you could be there to _____ [help us eat the food and drink the booze!/liven things up a bit!/organize the fun and games!]

Close with one of the following:

- RSVP, to____ [*name and phone number of host/hostess*]

- Only phone if you 're going to dis-appoint us.

- Will I see you then?

IN SICKNESS &
IN HEALTH

A priest sees people at their best, a lawyer at their worst, but a doctor sees them as they really are.

(Proverb)

The art of medicine consists of amusing the patient while nature cures the disease.

(Voltaire)

Never go to a doctor whose office plants have died.

(Erma Bombeck)

COMPOSING SYMPATHY NOTES

There is no "right" way to express sympathy over another person's loss. Each situation is different. But if you consider the following four questions while you write, your note will carry your sympathy and support to the bereaved.

- ◆ Where, when, or how did you hear the news?
- ◆ What was your immediate reaction?
- ◆ What thought, poem, or memory about the deceased can you share with the bereaved to convey your support or give comfort?
- ◆ How can you help?

Dear [*name*],

When Mary phoned and told me about Joe, I was stunned. This can't be true, I thought.

But as the reality of it began sinking in, my mind turned to memories of Joe. I remembered the time he offered to help Dad fix his car when it wouldn't start. Joe banged on the front fender with a big stick, claiming that the stick had "mechanical powers." Of course, we thought he was joking. But the car started! It wasn't til years later that he admitted he had snuck in the garage the night before and rewired the car properly.

Joe had a wonderful sense of humor and he was always so helpful. I shall miss him terribly.

In friendship and deepest sympathy,

P.S. If you don't feel like taking Rex for his walks right now, I would be more than happy to do it for you.

APPROPRIATE MESSAGES FOR SPECIFIC LOSSES

In some instances, you may want to use other people's thoughts and feelings about death if they are appropriate for the situation. If you do, I recommend including the author's name in the body of your note.

> Dear [*name*],
> I came across this quote of [author's name] and thought it might be of some comfort to you. Please accept my deepest sympathy and know that you are in my thoughts and prayers.

To someone who has lost a father:

> My father died many years ago, and yet when something special happens to me, I talk to him secretly not really knowing whether he hears, but it makes me feel better to half believe it.
>
> *(Natasha Josefowitz)*

To someone who has lost a mother:

> She knew that no human being is immune to sorrow and she wanted me to be tough, the way a green branch is tough, and to be independent, so that if anything happened to her I would be able to take hold of my own life and make a go of it.
>
> *(Ilka Chase)*

To someone who has lost a child:

> But the trees that lost their apples
> In the early windy year—
> Hard-cheeked little apples,
> Round and green and clear,—
> They have nothing more to lose
> And nothing more to fear.
>
> *(Frances Frost)*

To someone who has lost a spouse:

> The Buddha when dying was asked by his followers what they should do to maintain their practice after he was gone. He said, "Be a lamp unto yourself. Thus shall ye think of all this fleeting world: a star at dawn, a bubble in a stream; a flash of lightning in a summer cloud, a flickering lamp, a phantom, and a dream."
>
> *(Stephen Levine)*

> For she was beautiful — her beauty made
> The bright world dim, and everything
>   beside
> Seemed like the fleeting image of a shade.
> *(Percy Bysshe Shelley)*

To someone who has lost a friend:

> In this moment she felt that she had been robbed of an enormous number of valuable things, whether material or intangible: things lost or broken by her own fault, things she had forgotten and left in houses when she moved: books borrowed from her and not returned, journals she had planned and had not made, words she had waited to hear spoken to her and had not heard, and the words she meant to answer with...
>
> *(Katherine Anne Porter)*

PERSONALIZING QUOTES

Here is another quote about the death of a friend written by Antoine de Saint-Exupéry. Below, I've demonstrated how you can take wording from a quote and personalize it for your own situation.

> Bit by bit, nevertheless, it comes over us that we shall never again hear the laughter of our friend, that this one garden is forever locked against us. And at that moment begins our true mourning, which, though it may not be rending, is yet a little bitter. For nothing, in truth, can replace that companion. Old friends cannot be created out of hand. Nothing can match the treasure of common memories, of trials endured together, of quarrels and reconciliations and generous emotions. It is idle, having planted an acorn in the morning, to expect that afternoon to sit in the shade of the oak.
>
> *(Antoine de Saint-Exupéry)*

> Bit by bit, I'm beginning to accept the idea that Helen is no longer with us, that I shall never again hear the laughter of my friend. Nothing, of course, can replace the treasure of memories she and I had. But I find it comforting to remember how much we did share, the trials endured, the quarrels and reconciliations, and generous emotions. Old friends cannot be created out of hand. So I realize no one will ever mean to me what Helen has meant to me. To quote Antoine de Saint-Exupéry, "It is idle, having planted an acorn in the morning, to expect that afternoon to sit in the shade of the oak."

> With my sincerest sympathies, _____

USING PRINTS TO EXPRESS YOUR MESSAGE

Next time you're in a museum gift shop, pick up some cards with prints of famous paintings on them. There is a quality about certain artists' work, a beauty of expression that transcends time and sorrow. Here are two of my personal favorites with suggested messages of sympathy:

"Les Nympheas" by Claude Monet (1840-1926)

> Nothing I can say will ease the pain. But perhaps, every once in a while when the sadness washes over you, you'll look at these waterlilies and take comfort in them. I chose this print because if you examine it up close, all you see are brush strokes. Slashes of light blue. Dabs of yellow. A splotch of white. But if you look at the whole picture, it's peaceful. A resting place for anyone who cares to go there. Make it your resting place. For now. It's my gift to you.
> In sympathy and love,

"Interior with woman and cat" (detail) by Carl Holsoe (1863-1935)

> As the woman in this painting takes comfort from her cat, I hope and pray you'll find something to give you strength in the difficult days ahead. And if, like those squares of reflected sunlight, I can bring any warmth or brightness into your world right now, I am here.

COMFORTING WORDS
FOR THE BEREAVED PET OWNER

To animal lovers, the death of a pet is like losing a member of one's own family. Again, I'd recommend a simple opening about "not knowing what to say, hoping the following quote (and give the author credit) will be of some comfort," etc. Pick a card that is appropriate. Do not get one with an illustration that resembles the pet.

> **Animals are such agreeable friends — they ask no questions, they pass no criticisms.**
> *(George Eliot)*

> **An animal's eyes have the power to speak a great language.**
> *(Martin Buber)*

> **They called him Bull [*or substitute pet's name*] while he still lived, but now the silent parts of night possess his voice.**
> *(Tymnes)*

> **Macavity, Macavity, there's no one like Macavity,**
> **There never was a Cat of such deceitfulness and suavity.**
> *(T.S. Eliot)*

GENERAL CONDOLENCES

When you are writing a sympathy note to a business associate or someone you don't know very well, keep in mind that the gesture of doing it matters far more than what you write. If the person you're addressing isn't a close friend, you can't be expected to know what to say under the circumstances, so I recommend using a quote from William Shakespeare:

> **The worst is death, and death will have his day.**
>
> *(King Richard II)*

> **Men must endure**
> **Their going hence, even as their coming hither.**
>
> *(King Lear)*

> **This fell sergeant, death,**
> **Is strict in his arrest.**
>
> *(Hamlet)*

RHYMED CONDOLENCES

Some people prefer rhymed sympathy messages:

> **What can I say, but that it's not easy?**
> **I cannot lift the stones out of your way,**
> **And I can't cry your bitter tears for you.**
> **I would if I could, what can I say?**
>
> *(Rosalie Sorrels)*

> **Men die, but sorrow never dies;**
> **The crowding years divide in vain,**
> **And the wide world is knit with ties**
> **Of common brotherhood in pain.**
>
> *(Susan Coolidge)*

ANSWERING SYMPATHY NOTES

As difficult as finding the right phrase for a sympathy note may seem, answering those notes is not easy either. Some people choose to send a formal acknowledgment such as:

> **The family of [*deceased person's name*] thanks you sincerely for your kindness and sympathy at a time when it was deeply appreciated.**

Others opt for something more personal:

> **If God is good to me and I live a long life, I will always treasure your loving friendship during this difficult and frightening time.**

Sometimes, the simpler, the better:

> **Thank you for your kind expression of sympathy.**

You can substitute other appropriate words for kind, such as generous, heartfelt, timely, sincere, compassionate, or warm.

If writing any sort of sympathy acknowledgment seems totally overwhelming, why not share these feelings in your note? It will help to get it down on paper, and the recipient will no doubt appreciate your openness.

> **I can't begin to describe how tired I'm feeling. Even the simplest thing like fixing myself a cup of tea seems like an insurmountable task. That's why I haven't written sooner to thank you for your sympathy card. Hope you understand.**

GENERAL GET-WELL WISHES

If I had my way I'd make health catching instead of disease.

(Robert Ingersoll)

Everything is funny as long as it's happening to somebody else.

(Will Rogers)

To someone undergoing tests:

Your health comes first — you can always hang yourself later.

(Yiddish proverb)

To someone undergoing oral surgery:

The gums best understand the teeth's affairs.

(African proverb)

To someone undergoing cosmetic surgery:

**Vanity, vanity, all is vanity
That's any fun at all for humanity.**

(Ogden Nash)

To personalize a "get well" card, why not create a collage for the person you're sending it to? Suppose he's a ski enthusiast who has broken his leg and must remain in a cast for six weeks. Simply take a bunch of pictures from various ski magazines (people skiing, hopping over moguls, schussing down the slopes, etc.), paste them together in an interesting design, and include the words:

Get well soon so you can start being your old self again!

LONG-TERM ILLNESSES

Take some dried flowers and press them onto the outside of your card. An extremely helpful book in this art is *Dried Flowers For All Seasons*, by Betty Wiita. Then write:

> **Everything in creation has its appointed painter or poet and remains in bondage like the princess in the fairy tale 'til its appropriate liberator comes to set it free.**
>
> *(Ralph Waldo Emerson)*

Along the same lines, enclose some pine needles in a note with the following message:

> **I like trees because they seem more resigned to the way they have to live than other things do.**
>
> *(Willa Cather)*

> **(I'm here if you need me.)**

Find a greeting card that features someone painting, or sitting at a writing table. Then add these comforting thoughts:

> **Once we are able to get rid of our fears, once we have the courage to change from negative rebellion to positive nonconformism, once we have the faith in our own abilities to rise above fear, shame, guilt and negativity — we emerge as much more creative and freer souls.**
>
> *(Elizabeth Kübler-Ross)*

FOR THE CAREGIVER

It can be emotionally draining to care for someone with a long-term or terminal illness. During these times, notes of encouragement for the caregiver are vitally important.

God, give us grace to accept with serenity the things that cannot be changed, courage to change the things which should be changed, and the wisdom to distinguish the one from the other.

(Reinhold Niebuhr)

Of all the home remedies, a good wife is best.

(Kin Hubbard)

Be reverent towards each day. Love it, respect it, do not sully it, do not hinder it from coming into flower. Love it even when it is gray and sad.

(Romain Roland)

You will not grow if you sit in a beautiful flower garden. But you will grow if you are sick, if you are in pain, if you experience losses, and if you do not put your head in the sand, but take the pain and learn to accept it, not as a curse or punishment but as a gift to you with a very, very specific purpose.

(Elizabeth Kubler-Ross)

One by one the sands are flowing,
One by one the moments fall;
Some are coming, some are going;
Do not strive to grasp them all.

(Adelaide Proctor)

HOSPITAL HUMOR

Physicians of the Utmost Fame
Were called at once; but when they came
They answered, as they took their Fees,
There is no cure for this Disease.

(Hilaire Belloc)

A famous psychiatrist conducting a university course in psychopathology was asked by a student, "Doctor, you've told us about the abnormal person and his behavior; but what about the normal person?"
"If we ever find him," replied the psychiatrist, "We'll cure him."

(Anon.)

A hospital should have a recovery room adjoining the cashier's office.

(Francis O'Walsh)

One does not love a place less for having suffered in it.

(Jane Austen)

A wooden bed is better than a golden coffin.
(Russian proverb)

Definition of a doctor:

One upon whom we set our hope when ill and our dogs when well.

(Ambrose Bierce)

Definition of a cold:

An ailment cured in two weeks with a doctor's care, and in fourteen days without it.

(C.C. Furnas)

FOR THE NEWLY REFORMED

To the recovering alcoholic:

> **He who is master of his thirst is master of his health.**
>
> *(Proverb)*

To the ex-smoker:

> **Much smoking kills live men and cures dead swine.**
>
> *(George D. Prentice)*

> **No more coughing out your guts**
> **No more bumming half-used butts**
> **No more skin that's cracked and dry**
> **Your lungs say "thanks" and so do I!**
>
> *(JW)*

To the recovering substance abuser:

> **All dope can do for you is kill you... the long hard way. And it can kill the people you love right along with you.**
>
> *(From the movie* Lady Sings the Blues *based on the life of jazz singer Billie Holiday)*

To the successful dieter:

> **Tell me what you eat, and I'll tell you what you are.**
>
> *(Anthelma Brillat-Savarin)*

> **(You're lookin' good!)**

> **Wouldn't it be nice if two weeks on vacation seemed to last as long as two weeks on a diet?**
>
> *(Earl Wilson)*

To anyone who has made a change for the better:

> Habit is habit, and not to be flung out of the window by any man, but coaxed downstairs a step at a time.
>
> *(Mark Twain)*

> Of my own spirit let me be
> In sole though feeble mastery
>
> *(Sara Teasdale)*

> Discipline doesn't have to be about restriction, it can be about freedom, it can be about openness, it can be about more rather than less.
>
> *(Batya Zamir)*

> As a final incentive before giving up a difficult task, try to imagine it successfully accomplished by someone you violently dislike.
>
> *(K. Zenios)*

QUICK NOTES OF SUPPORT

Whether the person you are trying to cheer up is recuperating from an operation, adjusting to widowhood, or coping with a serious financial setback, the following phrases will express your support in a difficult time.

Things may look bleak right now. But somewhere down the road, as day follows night, there's an end to pain and uncertainty. I'm rooting for you!

This, too, shall pass.

May the Good Shepherd bring you comfort, hope, and cool, still waters to calm your troubled heart.

The way I look at it, your luck has GOT to change for the better. I'm keeping my fingers crossed for you!

"There is a time and season for everything under the sun." And there will be a time again for sunshine and laughter in your life.

Courage, my friend. Remember, what comes around, goes around!

MOVING UP &
MOVING ON

Work and thou canst not escape the reward; whether thy work be fine or coarse, planting corn or writing epics, so only it be honest work done to thine own approbation, it shall earn a reward to the senses as well as the thought. No matter how often defeated, you are born to victory. The reward of a thing well done is to have it done.

(Ralph Waldo Emerson)

Whenever a friend succeeds a little, something in me dies.

(Gore Vidal)

The little Road says, Go;
The little House says,
  Stay;
And oh, it's bonny here at
  home,
But I must go away.
(Josephine P. Peabody)

NEW JOBS

Your best friend finally found a great job she's really excited about. A coworker at the office has been promoted. The babysitter starts her very first 9-to-5 gig the day after tomorrow. Here are some bits of advice you may want to include in your congratulations or good-luck card:

For a first job:

> If you wish in this world to advance
> Your merits you're bound to enhance;
> You must stir it up and stump it,
> And blow your own trumpet.
> Or, trust me, you haven't a chance.
> (W.S. Gilbert)

> By working faithfully eight hours a day, you may eventually get to be a boss and work twelve hours a day.
> (Robert Frost)

> Success is that old ABC — ability, breaks, and courage.
> (Charles Luckman)

For a new job:

> Opportunities are usually disguised as hard work, so most people don't recognize them.
> (Ann Landers)

> Choose a job you love and you will never have to work a day in your life.
> (Confucius)

> The only person who had his work done by Friday was Robinson Crusoe!
> (Anon.)

ANAGRAMMED CONGRATULATIONS

An anagram is a puzzle in which you rearrange the letters of a word to spell something else. You can use this idea to offer your congratulations on a job promotion:

> INSIDE EVERY P-R-O-M-O-T-I-O-N THERE'S AN O-P-T-I-O-N!
>
> HERE'S TO THE JOB PRO (in) MOTION!

GENERAL JOB PROMOTION CONGRATULATIONS

> There is a thin line between genius and insanity: You have erased that line.
>> *(Oscar Levant)*

> Now that you've been promoted, you'll no doubt be "as busy as a one-armed man with the nettle-rash pasting on wall-paper."
>> *(O. Henry)*

> Everything comes to him who hustles while he waits.
>> *(Thomas A. Edison)*

> Promotion: new title, new salary, new office, same old crap.
>> *(Jim Fisk and Robert Barron)*

And for a female employee:

> The best man for the job is a woman.
>> *(Bumper sticker)*

NEW BUSINESS VENTURE

To achieve great things we must live as though we were never going to die.

(Marquis de Vauvenargues)

It takes 20 years to make an overnight success.

(Eddie Cantor)

A man isn't a man until he has to meet a payroll.

(Ivan Shaffer)

No bird soars too high, if he soars with his own wings.

(William Blake)

WHAT TO WRITE ON A GROUP CARD WHEN YOU'RE THE LAST TO SIGN

Keep walking and keep smiling.

(Tiny Tim)

Don't look back, something might be gaining on you.

(Satchel Paige)

Too much of a good thing is simply wonderful.

(Liberace)

RETIREMENT WISHES

I could be well content
To entertain the lag-end of my life
With quiet hours.

(Shakespeare)

How blest is he who crowns in shades like
  these,
A youth of labor with an age of ease.

(Oliver Goldsmith)

Every exit is an entry somewhere.

(Tom Stoppard)

Four rules for someone who is about to re-
tire:
1. Slip into it gradually, keeping your op-
tions open — after all, even race horses walk
to the starting gate.
2. Examine it from the point of view of how
it suits you, not your family's expectations
of what retired people should do or your
friends' plans for their futures.
3. Hold off any major financial commitment
until you know you like the lifestyle you've
planned.
4. Always keep in mind that key word to a
successful retirement: enjoy!

From a retiree to his or her successor:

It's time I stepped down for a less experi-
enced and less able man [woman].

(Professor Scott Elledge)

BUSINESS MOVES

To someone who is relocating:

> **To meet, to know, to love — and then to part,**
> **Is the sad tale of many a human heart.**
> *(Samuel Taylor Coleridge)*

> **You leave me much against my will.**
> *(Edna St. Vincent Millay)*

> **There is a Greek saying that goes: "The best things are most difficult." Even though the "best thing" for you is to move, the "most difficult" thing for me is to see you go. Good luck!**

To someone who is being transferred to another department write:

> **Sometimes, when one person is missing, the whole world seems depopulated.**
> *(Lamartine)*

> **(Even if you are only a few doors away!)**

To someone who is going on a leave of absence:

> **They say "Absence makes the heart grow fonder."**
> **...Yes, I know that duty calls.**
> **Just don't be gone**
> **For too damn long**
> **Or I'll start talking to the walls!**
> *(JW)*

To someone who's decided to quit, you could quote Heraclitus:

> **Everything flows and nothing stays.**

> **(Good luck! And here's to better days!)**

HAPPY GRADUATION!

ARISTOTLE REVISITED

"The roots of education are bitter, but the
    fruit is sweet."
I can't believe your schooling is *finally*
    complete!

(JW)

HORACE IN VERSE

"Instruction enlarges the natural powers
    of the mind."
— And also your powers of enjoyment.

It enlarges your circle of friends,
...And your chances of gainful
    employment!

(JW)

GET SERIOUS, PUBLILIUS SYRUS

"It is only the ignorant who despise
    education."
Here's to being smart, kid. Happy
    graduation!

(JW)

SOME DIFFERENT WAYS TO SAY "CONGRATULATIONS!"

Suggested greeting:

In Swedish it's "Grattis!" In Hebrew it's "Mazel tov!" However you say it, "Congratulations!" are in order.

More ways to congratulate someone in a foreign language:

Arabic:	**Mabrouk!**
Czech:	**Blahopráni!**
Dutch:	**Gefeliciteerd!**
French:	**Félicitations!**
German:	**Glückwünsche!**
Italian:	**Congratulazione!**
Japanese:	**Omedeto!**
Spanish:	**¡Felicidades!**
Yugoslavian:	**Čestitam!**

BAR/BAT(BAS) MITZVAHS

You're counted as an adult now
With new privileges and duties
Enjoy the things that living brings
Including all God's beauties.

(JW)

BAPTISM, CONFIRMATION,
AND FIRST HOLY COMMUNION

Be thou faithful unto death, and I will give
thee a crown of life.

(Rev. 2:10)

Faith without words is dead.

(James 2:26)

I never saw a Moor —
I never saw the Sea —
Yet know I how the Heather looks
And what a Billow be.
I never spoke with God
Nor visited in Heaven —
Yet certain am I of the spot
As if the Checks were given.

(Emily Dickinson)

Where there is communion there is something that is more than human, there is
surely something divine.

(Georges Duhamel)

To be baptized is to be born according to
Christ; it is to receive existence, to come into
being out of nothing.

(Nicolas Cabasilas)

HAVE A GREAT VACATION!

He who runs away and escapes is clever.
(African proverb)

The world is a book and those who do not travel read only one page.
(St. Augustine)

The advantage of travel is by seeing a great deal of both men and manners; it teaches us mutual toleration; and mutual toleration teaches us mutual love.
(Laurence Sterne)

For my part, I travel not to go anywhere, but to go. I travel for travel's sake.
(Robert Louis Stevenson)

My heart is warm with the friends I make,
And better friends I'll not be knowing;
Yet there isn't a train I wouldn't take
No matter where it's going.
(Edna St. Vincent Millay)

Remember "Old World Charm" usually means "no bathroom."
(Leonard Levinson)

TRAVEL TO SPECIFIC CITIES

According to the latest tourist business statistics, the top five most frequently visited cities in the world are Los Angeles, Madrid, Venice, Paris, and London. Here are some quotes you might want to include in a "Bon Voyage!" note to a friend who is planning to visit one or more of these places. (In this case, I would also recommend giving the original author credit.)

> **Los Angeles: Nineteen suburbs in search of a metropolis.**
>
> *(H.L. Mencken)*

> **Madrid: It may truly be affirmed that as God worked six days and rested on the seventh, Madrilenos rest the six [days], and on the seventh...go to the bull-fight.**
>
> *(H. O'Shea)*

> **Venice: It seems like being both in town and at sea, at one and the same time.**
>
> *(J.P. Cobbett)*

> **Paris: Nostalgia is the city's cheapest commodity and everyone foreign gets it for free.**
>
> *("Taki")*

> **London: When it's three o'clock in New York, it's still 1938 in London.**
>
> *(Bette Midler)*

HOW TO SAY
"HAVE A NICE TRIP!"
IN 12 DIFFERENT LANGUAGES

Suggested greeting:

To help you get in practice, let me wish you "Gutten reisen!" (Norway) and "Boa viagem!" (Portugal). By the time you get back, you'll know how to say "Have a nice trip!" in dozens of languages!

(Try to include foreign phrases from countries the person(s) will be visiting.)

To help you along, here's a list of ways to say "Have a nice trip!" in other tongues:

Arabic:	**Rehlah saeeda!**
Cantonese:	**Sun fung!**
Czech:	**Hezkou cesetu!**
Filipino:	**Maligayang paglalakbay!**
French:	**Bon voyage!**
German:	**Glückliche Reise!**
Italian:	**Buon viaggio!**
Spanish:	**Buen viaje!**
Russian:	**Shasleevava pootee!**
Turkish:	**Iyi yol culuklar!**

WELL-WISHES ON A NEW HOME

Bless the four corners of your little house
And be the lintel blessed,
And bless the hearth, and bless the board
And bless each place of rest.

(Arthur Guiterman)

It is when we pass our own private gate, and
open our own secret door, that we step into
the land of the giants.

(G.K. Chesterton)

On a humorous note, you might write:

As Miss America, my goal is to bring peace
to the entire world and then get my own
apartment.

(Jay Leno)

(Well at least you've accomplished the lat-
ter! Good luck!)

QUICK NOTES FOR
OFFICE OCCASIONS

In business situations, there will always be someone who is retiring, being promoted, going on maternity leave, etc. For these times, here are some general note ideas:

It's time you got on with the business of pleasure and forgot about the pleasures of business. Happy retirement!

"Slow and steady wins the race." Nobody deserves to win more than you do! Congratulations!

We'll all miss you, of course, especially me. But "doin' your own thing" is so important. Good luck! (And keep us posted, okay?!)

THANK-YOUS

If the only prayer you say in your whole life is "thank you," that would suffice.

(Meister Eckhart)

Gratitude is merely a secret hope of greater favors.

(La Rochefoucauld)

I cannot understand why I feel so embarrassed when being thanked. When thanks are at all profuse I get flustered, begin to wriggle and twist so that to cut things short I get rude.

(Bernard Berenson)

GESTURES OF KINDNESS THAT DESERVE
SPECIAL THANKS

A friend helps you move. A coworker supports you during an office shakedown. A next door neighbor offers to do your grocery shopping when she learns you have the flu. All these gestures of kindness deserve a special thanks. Here are some words you may want to add to your thank-you card:

To the person who helps you move:

> **A heavy burden does not kill on the day it is carried.**
>
> *(African proverb)*

> **(But I bet you were stiff the day after! Thanks again for helping me move.)**

To the loyal coworker:

> **When you are down and out, something always turns up — and it is usually the noses of your friends.**
>
> *(Orson Welles)*

> **(But not you, my friend. Thanks for being there when I needed your support.)**

To the helpful neighbor:

> **We can live without our friends, but not without our neighbors.**
>
> *(Scottish proverb)*

> **(Thanks again for your thoughtfulness.)**

> **After the verb "to love," "to help" is the most beautiful verb in the world.**
>
> *(Joseph Joubert)*

WHEN THANK-YOU NOTES ARE OBLIGATORY

According to *The New Emily Post's Etiquette Book,* there are certain times when you must send thank-you notes.

- ✉ After a dinner party, when you are the guest of honor.

- ✉ For birthday, anniversary, Christmas, and other gifts, when you have not thanked the gift-giver in person. (In some cases, as with close friends or relatives, a phone call is sufficient.)

- ✉ For shower gifts, if the gift-giver was not at the shower and/or you did not extend verbal thanks.

- ✉ For gifts given when someone is sick, thank-you notes must be sent as soon as he or she feels well enough to do so.

- ✉ Thank-yous should be sent for all sympathy notes except for printed cards with no personal message.

- ✉ When you receive congratulatory cards or gifts they should be acknowledged with a thank-you note.

- ✉ Wedding gifts. Even though verbal thanks have been given, all wedding gifts must be acknowledged within three months.

- ✉ Hostess gifts. Even though the gift is a thank-you itself, the hostess must thank her visitors in writing, especially if the gift has arrived by mail, so the visitor will know it has been received.

THANK-YOUS FROM AROUND THE WORLD

Next time someone you know deserves a special thank-you, why not dress it up with some words of gratitude from around the world?

In Hawaii, they say Mahalo, in Australia, it's Ta, but you deserve two whole words— Thank you! — for your incredible kindness.

(For other ways to say "thank you," see below.)

Arabic:	**Shokran**
Danish:	**Tak**
Dutch:	**Dank**
French:	**Merci**
German:	**Danke**
Greek:	**Efkaristo**
Italian:	**Grazie**
Japanese:	**Arigato**
Mandarin:	**Xiè xie**
Norwegian:	**Takk**
Portuguese:	**Obrigado**
Russian:	**Spaseeba**
Spanish:	**Gracias**
Swahili:	**Ashante**
Welsh:	**Diolch**

THE "THANKS-BUT-NO-THANKS"
THANK-YOU NOTE

It's always difficult to send a note thanking someone for something you secretly loathe and would like to exchange. If you find yourself in this position, here's a way of saying how you really feel without offending the giver:

> **I can't begin to describe how I feel about the present you gave me. Thanks so very much. I only hope I can return your gesture of kindness.**

PUBLIC THANK-YOUS

Sometimes, when there are a lot of people involved, a public thank-you notice in your local newspaper is a great way to save time and still express appreciation:

For a special wedding anniversary party:

> **We wish to express our thanks to all those unselfish people and organizations from whom we received cards and gifts on the occasion of our wedding anniversary. Sincerely,**

In response to replies received through a companion ad:

> **Box 5567 wishes to thank all the kind ladies/ sexy gents who responded to my ad of _____[date].**

SUGGESTED THANK-YOUS
FOR SPECIFIC OCCASIONS

To someone who has lent you money:

> **Generous people are rarely mentally ill people.**
>
> *(Dr. Karl Menninger)*

> **(Thanks for being so sane!)**

To someone who has bailed you out of a jam:

> **Like ice cream, our friendship**
> **Has so many flavors!**
> **And some day I hope to return**
> **All your favors!**
>
> *(JW)*

> **(Thanks again for your help.)**

To a gracious host and/or hostess:

> **Thanks for the meal,**
> **The great conversation,**
> **I look forward to next time**
> **With great anticipation!**
>
> *(JW)*

> **It isn't so much what's on the table that matters as what's on the chairs.**
>
> *(W.S. Gilbert)*

For a gift of liquor:

> **Sweet cyder is a great thing,**
> **A great thing to me,**
> **Spinning down to Weymouth town**
> **By Ridgeway thirstily.**
>
> *(Thomas Hardy)*

> **(What a shame old Tom Hardy isn't around to help me enjoy your generous gift. Cheers! And many thanks!)**

QUICK NOTE (WITH A QUOTE) FOR THANK-YOUS

Here it is folks, the all-purpose thank-you card! Whether you want to express your appreciation for a magnificently prepared seven-course dinner, or you want to acknowledge a generous contribution given to your favorite charity, the following suggestions will make writing thank-you notes so much simpler:

Dear [*name*],

_____[How can I possibly thank you enough for/There are no words to express how truly grateful I am for/ You're too kind! Thank you so much for] _____ [*describe gift*]

(Choose one of these quotes)

It says in the Bible, "God loves a cheerful giver." You certainly are one!

There's an old Danish proverb that goes, "He who gives to me teaches me to give." In that regard, my friend, you are one heck of a teacher.

If, according to *The Writings of Madame Swetchine*, "We are rich only through what we give," then you are, without a doubt, one of the wealthiest people in the world ...

(End with:)

Thanks again,
Gratefully yours,
Bless you for your kindness,

POSTSCRIPTS & AFTERTHOUGHTS

A postscript is the last notation on a letter.

> (Standard Handbook for
> Secretaries)

Dear, I thought I'd drop a
  line,
The weather's cool, the folks
  are fine;
I'm in bed each night at
  nine.
P.S. I love you.

> *(Johnny Mercer)*

af'ter thought' n. 1. an idea,
explanation, part, etc. coming or added later 2. a
thought coming too late to
be apt

> (Webster's New World
> Dictionary)

THE PURPOSE OF POSTSCRIPTS

One of the most neglected but effective note-writing devices is the P.S. or postscript (from the Latin words for "after" and "write"). P.S.'s can be used for a variety of purposes including:

Shock value:

> **P.S. — I'm pregnant!**

As a way of highlighting pertinent details:

> **P.S. My flight number is #3320 and it arrives next Tuesday at 3:32 p.m.**

To add something you found out after you finished writing your note:

> **P.S. Jane just phoned. She and Jim are moving to Australia!**

For a last-minute chuckle:

> **P.S. Where's my cigar?**

(Written at the close of a birth congratulations note.)

And, most frequently, to encourage a prompt reply:

> **P.S. Write soon!**

AFTERTHOUGHTS FROM THE AUTHOR

I've tried to cover all bases. There will be times, however, when nothing in this book seems particularly appropriate. What happens then? Whether you're writing a get-well card to a coworker, a thank-you note to your fiancé's mom, or a message of sympathy to a neighbor you hardly know, my final suggestion is to *find something you have in common with the person and mention it in your note*. Are you both cat lovers? Were you raised in the same part of the country? Do you share an interest in gardening? Whatever it is, include it. This will not only give you something to write about, it will also make the recipient feel "special."

> **Using quotes with your notes is the premise**
> **It's up to you now, Reader, to try it**
> **If the book works for you**
> **What I ask you to do**
> **Is tell all your friends to go buy it!**

(JW)

FOR FUTURE QUICK NOTES
AND FAST QUOTES

When you hear a great line or read a quote you simply must remember, here is some space to note down those clever words: Also, you might want to note down which quotes you have used for which occasions, so you don't send Aunt Agnes the same birthday quote twice!